CW00956917

The Hidden Treasure
in Suffering

By the same author:

The Hidden Treasure in Suffering

Shared from Personal Experience

Basilea Schlink

LAKELAND

LAKELAND
Marshall, Morgan & Scott
3 Beggarwood Lane, Basingstoke, Hants. RG23 7LP

Copyright ©Evangelical Sisterhood of Mary, 1985

Original title: *Zum Gewinn ward mir das Leid*
First German edition — 1983
First British edition — 1985

All rights reserved. No part of this publication may be reproduced, stored in a retrieval system, or transmitted in any form or by any means, electronic, mechanical, photocopying, recording or otherwise, without the prior permission of the copyright owner.

Unless otherwise stated, all Bible quotations are taken from the Revised Standard Version of the Bible, copyrighted 1946, 1952, 1971 and 1973, and used by permission.
Bible quotations identified AV are taken from the King James Version of the Bible, published by the Syndics of the Cambridge University Press, London.
Bible quotations identified GNB are taken from the Good News Bible — Old Testament: Copyright ©American Bible Society 1976, New Testament: Copyright ©American Bible Society 1966, 1971, 1976, and used by permission.
Bible quotation identified JB is taken from the Jerusalem Bible, copyrighted 1966 by Darton, Longman & Todd, Ltd. and Doubleday & Company, Inc.
Bible quotations identified LB are taken from the Living Bible, ©1971, Tyndale House Publishers, and used by permission.
Bible quotations identified RAV are taken from the Holy Bible: Revised Authorised Version, The New King James Version. Copyright ©1979, 1980, 1982, Thomas Nelson, Inc., Publishers, and used by permission.

British Library CIP Data
Schlink, Basilea
    The hidden treasure in suffering.
    1. Suffering—Religious aspects—Christianity
    I. Title II. Zum ward mir das Leid. *English*
    231'.8   BV4909
    ISBN 0-551-01239-0

Reproduced, printed and bound in Great Britain by
Hazell Watson & Viney Limited,
Member of the BPCC Group,
Aylesbury, Bucks

Contents

Suffering
is like a field
with buried treasure.
For hidden in suffering
are true joy and bliss,
divine life, waiting
to be discovered
by us.

1
Cares

You are engulfed by cares, which refuse to leave
you in peace at night. You are faced with a difficult,
complicated situation but can see no solution.
Mountains of cares loom before you, and you do
not know how to clear them away or where help
will come from. Perhaps the work load is depressing you. You are afraid that you are not going to
manage owing to lack of time and strength. Or you
are in financial straits. You may be concerned about
your children with their growing-up problems and
the difficulties they face in receiving a proper train-
ing for their future careers. You may be burdened
with cares arising from illness or worried about
your parents in their old age. These and a hundred
and one other cares may be weighing upon you.

Often our cares are, humanly speaking, justifi-
able. Even so, it may be good to first ask the Lord
for light. We ourselves may be to blame. Some
people lose themselves in worrying when their
wishes and demands are not fulfilled. They consider these particular desires to be essential to life,
whereas in fact they are not. People can grow very
frustrated when they do not attain a certain position they have been striving for in their career or
other areas of life. A simple question can help us
here: "Is it God's will that I be concerned about this
particular thing? Or am I worrying because I want

something that I am not supposed to have and that would not be beneficial for me?" How simply problems of this nature can be solved by surrendering our wills to God: "What God does not give me, I do not want to have. Because He is Love, He always leads me along the best path. If He had a better path for me, He would have led me along it."

However, there are cares on another plane which really are understandable, especially when they involve others entrusted to our care. These concerns can weigh heavily upon us. This I know from personal experience as spiritual mother of a sisterhood with approximately 200 Sisters, many of whom are stationed abroad — sometimes in distant countries — in 21 foreign branches. Because of the close links between the branches and the Mother House many difficulties and problems come my way — counselling matters, illness, problems of staffing, and so on, depending on the particular situation in the country concerned. In addition there are all the other matters arising at our headquarters, the little Land of Canaan, in West Germany. Thus day by day I am confronted with many problems and often do not know how they are to be solved.

Cares can be especially depressing if they magnify a particular suffering and its implications for the future. But the Lord showed me a solution for every mountain of cares, and that is the assurance that all the troubles and problems besetting us are part of an eternal counsel of God. As our loving Father, God has taken everything into consideration and led us into these difficulties. But at the same time He has planned the solution and a way out, for a true father never leaves his child without help.

As soon as I put my trust in this, I was able to give thanks and say, "You have the solution and so You will put it into my heart and mind when I now ask You to show it to me." For instance, whenever we came up with no solution during discussions about our ministry, I would repeatedly make a pause and pray to the Father in heaven for help, thanking Him at the same time: "You already have a solution to these problems and so You will show us the next step to solving them." Then — often very suddenly — a way would open up. This I can testify to, and with me our Sisters in positions of responsibility.

When faced with a difficulty, I would often begin to praise our heavenly Father, declaring what He is like: a Father who loves us and knows what we need. I would sing:

I will trust You, O my Father;
I'll believe and will not waver,
Knowing You have taken charge.

I will trust You, O my Father;
I'll believe and will not waver,
Knowing You will show the way.

I will trust You, O my Father;
I'll believe and will not waver,
Knowing You will help indeed.*

As I did so my heart would become joyful, filled with praise and thanksgiving that we have such a loving and caring Father in heaven. I knew that help and a solution would come — and they always did.

Perhaps you, too, have various responsibilities and are at a loss as to how you should act in certain situations, how you should advise your children, how you are to solve a particular difficulty, how to disentangle a complicated matter with many snags. Then why not try out the method that the Lord has shown me and that I have personally found to be so helpful? You will discover that mountains — in this case, mountains of cares — will melt like wax before the Lord (see Psalm 97:5). Yes, God is the Almighty One, who by uttering a single word can change everything: people and circumstances that may be creating difficulties, problems and troubles. All things are possible for God and He will do everything in His power to help us, for we are His children in Jesus Christ and He loves us. Often it is just a matter of having a little patience and waiting. But He will never be too late with His help.

When I have mountains of cares, the decisive factor is that I come as a child to God my Father. The Lord Jesus said in reference to the Father,

* Further requests can be inserted in this line.

Cares

"What father among you, if his son asks for bread, will give him a stone?" (Luke 11:11). If an earthly father will care for his child and if a man will help his friend when he is in need, how much more will our Father in heaven show goodness towards those who ask Him. If we trust in the Father's love and help, Jesus guarantees that we shall experience this, provided, of course, that we come and ask — yes, that we plead with Him like a child.

Once, many years ago, the Lord gave me this scripture in prayer at a time when our organization was in a very difficult situation and no human being could help us any longer. For many weeks we sang this verse every day after lunch: "What father among you, if his son asks for bread, will give him a stone? No father would do that!" (Not if he were a true father!) How much more could I count on our heavenly Father sending us the promised help. And He really did, although everything seemed utterly impossible. Like a miracle before our eyes, the mountain of cares was levelled.

When cares threaten to overwhelm us, we need to take God at His word, to make our stand on it and remind Him ever anew of His promise to help. "This is what You promised and Your name is Yea and Amen, so You will act accordingly. I shall experience that my troubles will be solved and all my cares will disappear! For what could be impossible for You? Nothing is impossible for You, even if humanly speaking there is no solution to my problem, no way out of my predicament."

God knows the way we are to go. He is able to help us in every situation and will make the promise of Holy Scripture come true: "Leave all your worries with him, because he cares for you" (1

Peter 5:7 GNB). Yes, He cares for us in every situation.

And so I would like to encourage you: Trust the Father. Stop circling round your cares. Pull the switch-lever. Instead of dwelling constantly upon certain difficulties, impossibilities, problems and people, and whatever else may be worrying you, keep thinking about the Father and what He is like and how, in His love, He is bound to help you and provide a solution.

Reverse the current of your thoughts and start giving thanks that God is your Father and that as His child you may go to Him and tell Him all about your cares. Then in the midst of problems and troubles you can say:

How I thank You, my Father!
Your help will surely come.
You will not leave me in the lurch
but provide a solution to my worries.
What a privilege to be a child of Yours,
whom You love and whom You will help
in Your good time!

2
Strained Relationships

You need help. Life has become unbearable for you because of strained relationships with others. Perhaps it is your marriage partner. Your children. Your colleagues at work. Or your neighbours. Whoever it may be, you are suffering immeasurably. You can see no solution, no way out. But for this suffering, too, God has prepared "spiritual medicine", which will bring help and healing. I have experienced this personally, and so have many others.

For a while I lived in the same house as a person who was known to be hysterical. Plagued with selfishness, envy and rebellion, this person made my life a misery, for she was incapable of seeing anything objectively or in its right perspective. Everything was twisted. Accusations and fits of rage were the order of the day. I could scarcely bear it any longer. Since this person spoilt everything for me, bitterness crept into my heart and I was almost tempted to give up trying. There was no way of communicating. A breach had arisen, and it seemed as though nothing could ever mend it. Everyone who realized what was happening assured me that nothing could restore this shattered relationship. But then in a miraculous way it was healed. I really experienced this. How did it happen?

One day, in my distress, I prayed fervently to the Lord for help. I asked Him what I should do so that a change would come about in this unbearable situation. Then, all of a sudden, it was as if the finger of God were pointing not at the other person, who was causing me such distress, but at me. "You are the one who has to change. You think it is all the other person's fault. It never occurred to you that it might also be your fault. Does not one of the main commandments say you should love your neighbour as yourself? Where is your love for this person? Is she not your neighbour, too? You no longer love her, and that is a sin against love. Nor is that all. You have even become resentful and are harbouring bitter thoughts, although the Bible says that bitterness, the refusal to forgive others, is one of the most serious sins and bars us from the Kingdom of God (cf. Matthew 6:15; 18:34f.; Hebrews 12:15). You are allowing Satan, the Accuser, to draw you over to his side, for accusations keep arising in your heart. You are guilty in the sight of God. You know that this person is rather unstable, whereas you are perfectly normal. You should have overcome this plight with the spirit of love and forgiveness. But you did not. Every time there was an angry outburst, you withdrew, and closed your heart."

It was as if Jesus went on to say: "As your Judge I am asking you today, Where is your forgiveness, your love? Love does not keep account of the wrongs that others do to it. I have not found a forgiving love in you, although you in your sins and failings constantly live from My forgiving love. So pray now that you will come to repentance over this great sin of unforgivingness and bitterness.

When your heart is filled with contrition, you will hasten to the foot of My cross and receive forgiveness through My shed blood. My blood will cleanse you at the same time, so that your hard heart will be softened, and love, instead of bitterness, will flow forth from it."

From that day onwards I prayed for a deep contrition. In the following weeks and months I would set aside about 20 minutes every morning for this request. In His mercy the Lord answered my prayer, and what He said came true: repentance drove me more than ever before to my Lord Jesus as a poor sinner, and I experienced that He did a new thing in my heart, giving me a merciful love for that person who made life so hard for me.

Then came another one of those especially trying days. I still remember the place where we were standing when once again an angry tirade descended upon me. Then, to my astonishment, I found myself reacting differently. Instead of closing my heart in defence, I could feel a compassionate love suddenly welling up within me. I took that person in my arms and gave her a kiss, so that she stopped and looked at me in amazement. From that day onwards things were never quite the same. No longer was our relationship beyond healing. No longer did it seem impossible or beyond hope that a bond of love would ever be forged. A new foundation had been laid. A change had taken place as on a revolving stage. It was no longer the other person but I who was at fault. Now I could ask forgiveness of her. Indeed, I felt constrained to do so. And this opened her heart. With the passing of time our relationship improved and that person underwent a complete transformation herself.

Again, what was the starting-point of this new relationship? Here the "principle of the revolving stage" was at work. If previously I see only what the other person is doing and how he has wronged me, all of a sudden the stage revolves and I see my own fault — I am the guilty one.

It is certain that you will experience the same when you cry to the Lord in your distress, for He is the same God and Father. If you do not cease to pray faithfully for a contrite heart, He will hear your prayer and give you repentance. Your relationship with the other person will undergo a transformation.

In retrospect you will see that your difficulties in getting on with another person actually brought you something very precious. Indeed, suffering always brings precious things with it. First, your distressing situation opened your eyes to your sinful nature, and the truth sets us free — free from the great sin of self-righteousness, free from resentment and bitterness, free from pharisaism, which always puts the blame on others. Thus the traumatic experience of a shattered relationship brings us close to our Lord Jesus, for nothing so unites us with Jesus and the Father as when we come to the cross as penitent sinners. Then there is joy in the heart of God, and He causes this joy to flow into our hearts. In His love Jesus draws near to the soul that humbly acknowledges his sins before God and his fellow beings. He fills us with joy and peace, whereas previously when we were still accusing the other person we were unhappy and inwardly torn.

Yes, we can only praise God for letting us reach the end of our resources in our relationship with others and for giving us light to see our sin and guilt. Then we come to know Him in His infinite compassion, love and forgiveness. Through this suffering God wants to give us the most precious gift He can possibly give us, the gift of love. If He can fill our hearts with love, merciful love, for our neighbour who is a burden to us, we shall become the happiest ones of all; for nothing can make us so happy as loving others, including those who hurt us. As loving souls we shall then enter His kingdom of love and glory in heaven above rather than being barred from it. So what do we gain from the suffering of having to live with a difficult person? — Immeasurable blessing.

3
Fear

You suffer from fear. You are tormented, hounded, by fear. Fear ruins everything for you — the blessings you have received and everything else that you might otherwise have enjoyed. Perhaps you have visions of calamity lurking on all sides, ready to descend upon you and your loved ones, and you are afraid: afraid of serious illnesses or of bankruptcy as a result of the economic situation and the growing precariousness of our existence; afraid of burglaries, muggings, acts of violence and terrorism, which are now daily occurrences; afraid of demonic powers, curses and spells with their terrible effects; afraid of uprisings, street battles, famine; afraid of impending persecution against Christians; afraid of a nuclear war.

Jesus Himself says, "Here on earth you will have many trials and sorrows" (John 16:33 LB). He prophesied for the end times, which have already begun, that men will be "dying of fear as they await what menaces the world" (Luke 21:26 JB). Yes, fear can cost us our health. Fear can be fatal. It is an established fact that shock and fear are a frequent cause of death in traffic accidents.

How can we overcome this suffering, this great malady of fear, especially if we are fearful by nature?

May I share with you how as a fearful person I

18

overcame my fear. During the Second World War I served with a missionary society as a travelling lecturer, and my travels took me throughout Germany. Often I experienced air raids, even coming under the fire of low-flying aircraft. When fear rose in my heart, there was a short prayer that helped me: "For You, Jesus! It's for You that I'm doing this ministry, which involves so many dangers!" As I committed myself to God's leadings, I could sense His nearness, and all fear was banished.

Then came the Cuba crisis in 1962. There was a considerable stir and a general scare that this spark would set the whole world on fire. In their fear people came to us from other areas, looking for some kind of security. I still recall the feeling of fear that welled up in me, too: "What if another world war breaks out now? It will be far more terrible than the last one." This time I had others to think of, for I was responsible for a large family of Sisters. (Is it not true that our fear about coming hard times is often magnified not so much because of ourselves as because of our loved ones?) Yet once again my fear was dispelled by the sense of Jesus' presence and the assurance that "Naught can befall me [and those close to me] that He did not choose and that would not serve to my ultimate good."*

Fear is justified only if we have ruled Jesus Christ out of our way of thinking and our faith. But if we allow Jesus to step into those frightening situations we have been envisioning, then all of a sudden everything will be different. There will no longer be that terrible sense of inevitability. Jesus will break through our preconceived notions and the cycle of

* Words of a German hymn.

fear in which we are caught up. We may rest in the assurance that He is present. Just as He drew near to His fearful disciples long ago, He will draw near to us, saying, "Peace be with you" (John 20:21). At these majestic words His peace flows into our hearts and we are uplifted. We need to believe that the trouble and misery we were dreading will not unfold automatically in all their terribleness, but that the Lord will overrule — He who is so different from us and our way of thinking. In the measure that we believe this, in that measure we shall experience His transforming power.

Jesus comes to us as a Light to lighten the darkness and as the Prince of Peace to give us peace and drive fear away. He draws near to us as our Helper and helps us in our distress. If the thing we dreaded comes to pass, Jesus Christ is on the scene to help us, for that is love's way. He deals with us in accordance with His almighty power. In peril and misery He can give us the aid we need and grant us miraculous instances of His protective care when no one else can help us. When He is near us, we shall experience the reality of the Psalm verse, "Though I walk in the midst of trouble, thou dost preserve my life; thou dost stretch out thy hand against the wrath of my enemies, and thy right hand delivers me" (Psalm 138:7).

Fear will turn into courage if we believe that Jesus will come to us in the midst of our fear. This is what happened to the disciples on the Sea of Galilee as the waves threatened to engulf them and they cried out for fear. Suddenly Jesus was with them and saying, "Take heart, it is I; have no fear" (Matthew 14:27). It is like a command: "Fear not. You treat My love with disdain if you are afraid.

You act as if I would not take care of you when you are in distress." To us, too, Jesus is saying, "Take heart!" He hastens to those who are in distress and peril. Yes, when the surging waves are at their peak, Jesus will come — He who commands the waves and takes the ship's helm into His own hands. With a strong arm He then guides us safely over the waves. No one loves us so dearly as our Lord Jesus Christ. Should He not, therefore, be capable of driving away our fear?

Are we afraid of a particular suffering coming into our lives? Fear can dominate us only to the degree that we are unwilling to accept such hardships and to say, "Yes, Father." Our lack of dedication comes from our not trusting in the love of God the Father, who will never let us be tempted beyond our powers of endurance (see 1 Corinthians 10:13). "There is no fear in love" (1 John 4:18). On the other hand, if we have the right kind of fear, a godly fear and reverence for the holy God, then our agonizing fear and dread of coming events will disappear. Then we are no longer afraid of the coming sufferings and of the harm people might do to us, but rather of grieving the Lord and losing Him by disregarding His commandments or by failing to bring sin into the light in order for it to be cleansed. If we lose God, we lose everything. If we have God, we have everything we need — even in the hardest times. "If God is for us, who is against us?" Then we can declare in triumph like the Apostle Paul, "Neither death, nor life...nor things present, nor things to come...will be able to separate us from the love of God" (Romans 8:31-39).

Thus in times of fear — in everyday life and in view of a perilous future — our primary concern

should be that God can be for us because we are
walking in the light and living in a state of contrition and repentance, ever conscious of God's holiness. Then, in a new and deeper way, we shall
come to know and love God as our merciful Father
and Jesus as our Saviour. And if I love someone, I
trust him. Jesus promised, "He who loves me will
be loved by my Father...If a man loves me, he will
keep my word...and we will come to him" (John
14:21,23). In other words, God will then come to us,
and His coming marks the solution to all our problems.

The fact remains that fear is a type of suffering.
However, divine joy and blessing lie hidden in
every form of suffering — and fear is no exception.
Peace surpassing all understanding, peace flowing
like a river from God's heart into ours and filling us
with delight — this is to be ours when fear attacks
us. Jesus is our peace. Because He feels especially
obliged to come to us in such times of fear, we shall
taste this peace as never before. It is a foretaste of
what it will be like in the City of God, the city of
everlasting peace, where no more fear or distress
can approach us.

He who is peace itself wants to give you this
wonderful peace as a gift. You can trust Him. And
when you are faced with fear and peril, this is the
very moment to claim this precious gift in faith.

4
Illness

You are ill. Your body is racked with pain. Emotionally you are suffering too, for this illness has more or less removed you from your family life, your activities and whatever else brought you fulfilment. You long to work but cannot. You are impeded in everything. Once you had the satisfaction of doing something meaningful with your life, perhaps helping others and bringing them joy, or even building up a ministry. Now all this is no longer possible. You have become a burden to others. You are dependent on their help and need to be waited on. Now all of a sudden your life consists of pain and suffering. You are denied the full and active life of a healthy person.

Perhaps time and again you set your hopes on being cured. You were put in touch with a good doctor for treatment or prescribed a special medicine. Or perhaps you prayed a great deal for recovery, hoping that our Lord Jesus would be your Healer and that in accordance with James 5:14 and 15 you would be healed through prayer and the laying on of hands. But so far all your hopes were dashed.

Yet should not a precious treasure also lie hidden in illnesses for which there is no cure in sight, illnesses that we can only suffer in patience? Yes. Indeed, it cannot be otherwise. For if our suffering weighs heavy, so does the blessing it contains.

This we can see from the life of the American Joni, who owing to a diving accident became a quadriplegic. After complicated surgeries and long stays in hospital, she was confined to life in a wheelchair while still in her teens, and is totally dependent on the help of others. As a result of all this she came to a deeper faith in Jesus Christ and by saying Yes to the will of God she has triumphantly overcome this severe suffering. The story of her life has been printed and filmed, and so her testimony travels around the world: "I'd rather be in this chair, knowing Him, than on my feet without Him."* You have to take her word for it that she is happy, for she is radiant, thus glorifying the Lord. Yes, what joy enters our lives when Jesus means everything to us! The ordeals of illness grow small in comparison.

The important thing is that God is glorified in our lives. This can happen in various ways. Through prayer and the laying on of hands God can suddenly grant us healing, as I have experienced a number of times. But there were also times when the Lord did not intervene and I had to taste the bitter dregs of the cup of illness. In such cases the Lord is glorified in that we bear our illness in complete submission to Him, as we can see from the story of Joni. This will result in the greatest blessing for ourselves and others, showing forth who God is and what He can do. And in this way He can call many to Himself.

What was it that comforted me during a serious illness that kept me imprisoned in my room for months on end and usually on my own because the

* From the film *Joni* by World Wide Pictures.

doctor had ordered absolute quiet and few visitors?
What was it that brought me an unforgettable blessing? Hanging on the wall opposite my bed was a
crucifix. It was as if Jesus, the crucified Lord, were
saying to me, "Did you not commit yourself to following Me on the way of the cross? I am the Man of
Sorrows, afflicted and covered with wounds. Now
you have the chance to go with Me and to open
your heart to My sufferings in a new and deeper
way." During this period of illness Jesus drew
closer than ever as the Man of Sorrows. My love for
Him grew, and so, too, my thanksgiving for His
sufferings. The Lord led me into a deeper and more
loving union with Himself. From that time onwards I was far more closely knit to His will and
thus united with His heart. I discovered what a
blissful thing that is. Yes, this long period of illness
taught me to surrender my will anew to Him, week
by week, and to practise being patient when there
was still no sign of improvement.

Illness is a refining process. The Father sends it
to us with the request, "Practise patience now, and
later you will be able to endure patiently in all kinds
of trouble and suffering. You will grow strong by
dedicating and rededicating your will to God, and
you will be changed into the image of Jesus, the
ever patient Lamb of God, whose food was to obey
the will of God."

How thankful I was later for this opportunity of
practising patience! We shall be able to remain at
peace in distressing situations to the extent that we
have learnt to be patient and to submit our will to
God in the assurance that His heart and will are nothing but loving-kindness and that the paths He
leads us on are always good. Then we shall have

risen above the difficulties, knowing that the blessing of God and glory lie hidden in them. Because
God is Love, He has plans to do us good and not to
harm us (see Jeremiah 29:11). Everything, including illness, is meant to serve to our ultimate good,
and this happens when our will is surrendered to
God. Then He can grant us that which He has intended for us. When there is no rebellion — that is,
no resistance on our part — there is nothing to prevent His blessing from flowing down upon us.

Severe illnesses that bring us face to face with
death are of great significance and rich in blessing,
as I discovered repeatedly in our family of Sisters.
For some of my spiritual daughters it was God's
plan that their illness should lead to death. Despite
prayer and the laying on of hands, the Lord did not
intervene, for He intended to call them home.
However, He used their time of severe illness to
prepare them for their departure from this life; and
with them we were then privileged to experience
something of the inexpressible glory of heaven.

Weeks before her death one Sister was so radiant
that everyone entering her sickroom could hardly
believe it. The presence of heaven was almost tan-
gible. Not only we but visitors were amazed at
what the Lord had accomplished here. The
radiance that lay upon another Sister was so great
that after her death the undertaker, who had seen
countless numbers of dead persons over the years,
commented in astonishment, "How happy the Sister looks!" The joy of being with Jesus in the
heavenly glory already shone from her face 20 minutes before her death and still lay on her features
after she had passed away.

To be sure, these Sisters had prepared themselves all their lives in contrition and faith to meet the Lord when their last moment came, but it was their critical illness — for some it lasted months or even years, and for others only a few weeks — that brought them the final spiritual preparation. Thus the heavenly glory shone forth at their death — and most important of all — we know that they are there where the overcomers see Jesus face to face. They are with Him for ever.

What blessings lie hidden in the trials of illness! How many people have testified that so long as they were well, they were wrapped up in their work, their families, daily events, having little fellowship with the heavenly Father and our Lord Jesus Christ throughout the day. Or they may even have been very far away from the Lord. Then came a period of illness, perhaps a time of severe suffering, when they were laid up, and all of a sudden there was an encounter with God. The patient found himself confronted with the holiness of God, especially if he had to reckon with his death. There was a spiritual awakening in his life, a conviction of sin, a realization that he had strayed from God and had not lived as a disciple of Jesus in thought, word and deed. This awareness was followed by contrition and repentance, which led to confession of sin, a change of heart, yes, even a total renewal of the person's life. How many people have said, "It's all thanks to the sufferings that God gave me to bear. This illness has brought me untold blessing."

Apart from that, we shall experience in some measure the reality of the scripture, "When your body suffers, sin loses its power" (1 Peter 4:1 LB). When we are laid up, we are not only convicted of our sins more than at any other time, but often the suffering parts of our bodies are those with which we sinned. We can no longer talk much — and what did we previously use our tongues for? One day we shall have to give account for every careless word we uttered (see Matthew 12:36). We can no longer get about on our feet, going where we like. But where did we hurry to when we were on our feet? Often to places where God did not want us to go. And what did we use our hands for? Often just to get something done for ourselves or our families. But time and again we failed to bear in mind that we should do everything out of love for our Lord Jesus and to His glory.

During times of illness we may suddenly be faced with the words of Holy Scripture: "Whatever a man sows, that he will also reap" (Galatians 6:7) — reap for all eternity. God is not mocked. If we allow the Holy Spirit to guide us in our work and in every other area in our lives, we shall reap everlasting joy in heaven and receive a glorious reward. But if we follow the dictates of our human nature, indulging in the desires of the flesh and persisting in various sins (see Galatians 5:19-21), we shall harvest ruin. What a blessing, then, is a time of illness, for it gives us another chance to repent before it is too late.

Yet times of illness are not only intended to work repentance in our hearts. There is more to it. As already mentioned, the trials of illness are meant to draw us closer to Jesus. This can also happen when we experience that others grow annoyed with us because we have become a burden to them. Or some may forget us, although we used to be close friends or fellow workers. That hurts. We realize how quickly human love fades away. But then the

Lord Jesus stands before us, entreating us: "Turn to Me more fully, seek Me, and in Me you will find all that your heart longs for." Jesus came so that in Him we may have life in all its fullness (see John 10:10). The trials of illness can teach us to love Jesus more, and then we shall taste more of His love.

There seems to be no end to the treasures that lie hidden in illness. When we ourselves are ill and suffer bodily, we grow more compassionate and have a greater understanding for others who are also sick and feeling poorly. Moreover, what a blessing and encouragement sick people have been with their intercessory prayer, spiritual counselling, advice and testimonies! In the crucible of solitude they drew closer than ever to the heart of God, and thus they had more to give. Indeed, many a sickroom has become a spiritual oasis for its surroundings.

Yes, illness is a form of suffering, often a severe one, but for this very reason — as we were saying — the blessing, too, is very great, and precious gems lie hidden in it. How apt are the words of that German hymnist: "O suffering, who is worthy of you? Here you are called a burden, above you are called an honour that is not granted to everyone" (K.F. Harttmann). Even in this life a sick person who lovingly accepts the will of God can have a foretaste of heaven, and in the life to come everlasting glory awaits him.*

* For further reading: Basilea Schlink, *The Blessings of Illness*.

5
Weariness

You say, "I've almost reached the limit of my endurance. All my strength has gone. I'm too tired to think or do anything. I can barely drag myself through the day." This exhaustion and frailty may be the residuals of an illness or the results of old age. But nowadays even young people are weary and lacking in strength. Is it not true that negative environmental factors and the detrimental influences of modern society are telling on the rising generation? Compared with the past, young people today are often physically weaker.

Such a state of exhaustion is wearing and sometimes harder to bear than illness, especially if it is prolonged and yet, unlike a sick person, we cannot be excused from our daily obligations at home or at work. How you long to be active like others, in full possession of your strength! Perhaps you have already prayed a lot that the Lord would take away your physical weakness or you may have tried various external aids to gain strength but with no success. Your weariness will not go away.

I am familiar with this kind of condition and know how trying it can be. But I have also learnt to triumph over this condition and discovered what a precious treasure God has hidden in this suffering, too. For many years now I have suffered from various ailments and delicate health. Often I just did not know where I was to find the strength to tend to the many tasks facing me in the leadership of our expanding organization. Considering my frailty, how was I supposed to carry out this large, worldwide ministry, which brings with it an abundance of work each day? I could hardly cope any longer.

In this situation Jesus helped me by giving me something which proved to be a great source of strength in my frailty. He drew my attention to a verse in Holy Scripture, making it come true in my life in a wonderful way: "My grace is sufficient for you, for my power is made perfect in weakness" (2 Corinthians 12:9). This scripture which, one could say, became my very own evoked a song of triumph in my heart: "If Your power is actually made perfect in weakness, why should I mind being weak? Then You will show forth Your power in me and through me, and Your power is far greater than my strength. What a tremendous promise!"

Filled with thanksgiving, I said to the Lord, "Now You want to make Your strength effective in me. I no longer have to rely on my little strength and limited resources." In faith I clung to the Lord's promise. When I was then barely able to cope any longer, I always found it a help to repeat a few words such as, "Jesus, my Strength!" or: "There is power in Your blood!" And every time I was infused with new strength — His strength!

For those who are suffering from fatigue and poor health, what a comfort it is to know that Jesus wants to make us a gift of His strength, which is sufficient for us, yes, more effective than if we were strong in ourselves. Therefore, let us say, "Lord

Jesus, I am trusting and expecting You to do this!" If we declare in faith ever anew, "Jesus, my Strength!" then we shall actually be pervaded by a current of divine life proceeding from Him, the risen Lord. This is a promise that we can also claim for the future. In the coming time of distress, when afflicted with physical weakness, we may reckon with the power of God.

What a wonderful experience is ours as a result of this particular suffering! Who would not want to accept weariness and physical weakness if the Lord's strength is to be so wonderfully demonstrated in us? We shall come to know Jesus as our mighty Lord and learn to trust and love Him more, entering a deeper union with Him. This I experienced ever anew during times when I was feeling weary. It was as if a melody were gently ringing in my heart over and over again: "My Lord Jesus, now I have the privilege of making a small sacrifice for You by doing my work when it costs me something. Now You are giving me the chance of proving my love for You and being close to You." Thus a great blessing lies hidden in this suffering too — an abundance of deep inner joy. Love, nothing but love — this is what our heavenly Father and our Lord Jesus are like! The bigger our cross, the greater the glory it shall produce, and even in this life we shall experience something of heaven.

6
Loneliness

You are all alone, and loneliness is gnawing at your heart. It's almost more than you can bear. Death has taken away from you the one you love, the one who meant everything to you, and now you are all on your own. Or your marriage has broken up and you are left behind with an aching heart. Or you are single and living by yourself with no friends who lovingly surround you. Or you are elderly. Hardly anyone cares about you. No one seems to want or need you.

Whatever the cause may be, you have to taste the bitter herbs of loneliness. I can feel for you, having also gone through times of loneliness.

In the early nineteen-fifties while I was leading an active, meaningful life as a spiritual mother loved and needed by a large family of Sisters, the Lord suddenly called me to a life of solitude. For His sake I was to give up this happy fellowship and spend months in seclusion for many years, devoting myself entirely to the Lord in prayer and writing down what He commissioned me to share as a spiritual testimony. For this purpose I was to remain alone in my room, separated from my loved ones. I gave the Lord my consent to this leading, little realizing how hard loneliness is. Now there was no one to talk things over with. Now I was no longer happily united with my spiritual daughters as before — singing, worshipping, celebrating festivals of heaven, and so forth. Now I was no longer present when important decisions were discussed concerning our Sisterhood and ministry. I was all on my own behind four walls. And when the Lord Jesus also seemed far away from me, loneliness would gnaw at my heart.

Like many of my brothers and sisters in the Lord who are all alone, though for other reasons, I had to drain the cup of loneliness. I know how loneliness can crush the heart and almost kill you. Loneliness is like a wild beast that pounces on you and tries to devour you. You feel like rattling the iron bars of your "prison" and escaping from your lonely existence.

Then there was an incident that helped to turn this suffering into gain for me and bring about something wonderful. How did this path of loneliness become a precious gift for me? One day it was as if the Lord were saying to me, "You long for the love of people and for fellowship with them. Love Me all the more, and you will bring comfort and joy to My heart; and by showing Me love you will become all the happier and your life will be the richer for it." And so I started singing songs of love to our Lord Jesus. How lonely He is! — forsaken, rejected, unloved by us, the sons of men, for whom He laid down His life out of love. With songs like the following I sought to console His heart.

My Jesus' heart must be consoled
Today in all His grief untold.
Awake, my soul, begin to sing —
What comfort has your love to bring?

I'll comfort Him, with Him abide,
In suff'ring always at His side,
No single hour forsaking Him.
Perhaps this will then comfort Him.

I'll comfort Him by gratefully
Recounting all He's done for me,
By thanking Him for all His love.
Oh, can His heart now still be grieved?

I'll comfort Him, His heart delight
With songs of love in deepest night.
Such steadfastness would touch His heart
And comfort sweet to Him impart.*

In so doing, I was greatly comforted myself. Jesus drew near to me, and in the solitude I had true communion with Him. Not even in the most spiritual times of fellowship with others had I experienced such deep joy.

Nor was that all. At that time I had no idea that this communion with Him, which I was privileged to experience at the cost and loss of human fellowship, would bring blessing to others, for sacrifice brings forth life, divine life. I was able to share some of the things that Jesus revealed to me in times of seclusion. Being alone was no longer a sacrifice but a gift that I could give to Jesus as a token of my love. Peace and joy now filled my heart.

We are all meant to experience this in one form or the other, for the Lord in His love has planned pathways of loneliness for us, not so that our hearts

* See Basilea Schlink, *I Want to Console You — Songs of Love and Comfort for Our Lord in His Suffering Today*.

will be tormented or embittered, but so that we shall seek Him and draw closer to Him. Jesus is waiting to be found by us. He will give Himself to us and our hearts will find abundant peace and joy in Him. Every pathway that God, our loving Father, leads us on is part of a wise plan and brings us to a wonderful goal. We shall receive far more in return for everything we forsook on His account and taste the love of Jesus all the more abundantly.

There is only one thing you need to do: give Jesus your love. Jesus longs for your love. He loves you dearly and is waiting for you to love Him in return. Love Him, and your loneliness will be transformed into communion with Him and will bring you everlasting joy one day above. As a result of your communion with Jesus, you will find ways of showing love to others — for instance, by praying for them — and you will have no more time to think about how lonely you are without the love of others. If you love Jesus and your fellow beings, your life will become fruitful, and one day you will go home to the Lord with a bountiful harvest.

7
Inner Conflict

You are suffering from great inner conflict, because you can no longer understand God's leadings and actions. Your soul cries out in anguish, "Why is God silent? Why doesn't He intervene in my life and send help? Why is everything so meaningless? Why is it that in world affairs nowadays evil is increasingly triumphant?"

Perhaps you have agonizing doubts about whether your sins are really forgiven. You may be in a quandary about whether you have made the right decision, whether you dealt with a person in the right way, whether you followed the right course of action in a particular situation. All these doubts prey on your mind. Inner conflict holds you captive as in a vicious circle, making your spirit and soul suffer immeasurably.

As your loving Father, God does not want you to torment yourself with these doubts. He wants to help you find your way out of this vicious circle, so that you can overcome your inner conflict and one day receive the crown of life, which is promised those who have stood the test (see James 1:12).

It is a fact, as I know from my counselling experience, if you give way to inner conflict, if you keep agonizing over unsolved problems, you will never arrive at a solution. On the contrary you will find yourself even more entangled, and your tormenting thoughts will drive you to the edge of despair.

But the Lord shows us the decisive step that will lead us out of this suffering: to call a halt to all these agonizing thought-processes and to renounce them in Jesus' name and — every time they come back — to reject them categorically. Yes, we need to rebuke them in the name of Jesus: "I refuse to have anything to do with these thoughts that the Enemy has planted in my mind! Begone! God will help me. He will show me what is right." Ever anew we need the resolution to step out of the vicious circle of our own thoughts and to turn to Someone else: Jesus Christ.

For you, too, the next step is to bring before Jesus all your inner conflict. Talk everything over with Him. Pray to Him. Jesus is waiting for you to turn to Him, for as it is written, "Resist the devil and he will flee from you. Draw near to God and he will draw near to you" (James 4:7f.). At the same time we can claim the help of Jesus. Having been tempted as we are but without sinning, He can help us when we are tempted (see Hebrews 2:18; 4:15). As our great High Priest, He has compassion on us and wants to help us. But we also have to believe that He has the answer and solution. They are bound to come, for God, who alone is wise and almighty, has a solution prepared for every problem that you do not know how to solve. And because God loves you, He will not leave you in suspense as to whether you have made the right decision in a particular situation or as to how you should decide and act in another case. He is the Light and the Truth, and so He will guide you into all the truth. This I have experienced time and again in my life when I was faced with many important decisions and was unsure what to do because of the contradictory advice I received.

If you are tormented with doubts as to whether you have made the right decision, are on the right track, or have dealt with someone the right way, then take your stand on the Scripture verse, "He leads me on the right path for his name's sake" (Psalm 23:3 according to the German Luther Bible), which can also be applied to times of inner conflict. Whenever I was threatened by inner conflict, I clung to this verse, and my agonizing thoughts left me when I said to the Lord, "If a child asks his father to show him the right way to go, the father won't let him go the wrong way without immediately calling him back." How much more so our Father in heaven. You can rely on that. If you surrendered your will completely to the Lord beforehand and asked Him to show you the right way to go and the right decision to make, you can trust that He has guided you in your decisions. If the Enemy keeps on trying to entangle your thoughts in his net, say ever anew, "My Father, who loves me, will not allow me to go the wrong way. And so my decision was right. And if it had been wrong, He would have shown me very clearly."

However, you may be in a quandary because you did not specifically ask God for guidance before making a decision. Perhaps you even acted in self-will. And now the situation preys on your mind. Then the next step is to bring your sin to Jesus in contrition. If you are truly sorry and ready to repent and — whenever possible — to make amends, the Lord Jesus will say to you, "You are forgiven this sin!" He sees your humble, contrite heart, and you can trust that He will then cover with His precious blood all the consequences of your sinful, self-willed decision. Your inner conflict will yield and He will grant You His peace.

Now, there is a special kind of inner conflict that arises when we have to follow a difficult path that seems meaningless to us. Again, you need to realize that you cannot solve this problem by yourself. Help can come only from the Lord, whose thoughts are infinitely higher than ours (see Isaiah 55:9), who is totally different from us and who in His wisdom, omnipotence and immeasurable love can and desires to bring you the solution. God's footsteps are hidden, as it were, in deep waters. You can neither see them nor make out where they are going. But one thing is certain: the Lord is leading you unerringly to a very wonderful goal.

So do not puzzle over God's leadings and ask why He is taking you along a path that seems meaningless to you, a path that leads through darkness and confusion, a path whose outcome is hidden from you. Trust Him instead. Know that He is the omniscient, all-loving and everlasting God, your Father, whose heart is nothing but love and whose will is the essence of goodness. Even though you feel as though you were wandering in a maze, He is guiding you according to a wise and eternal counsel and leading you on to a wonderful goal. God, who is Love and Truth, would never lead a child of His into a maze, and so He cannot be leading you into a maze. It only seems like that to you. Put your trust in Him, wait a while, and you will see that this seemingly meaningless path has a deep meaning to it. God is preparing an outcome that will fill you with awe and wonder, for with Him suffering is never the end.

Instead of wallowing in doubts and temptations and letting them torment you, board the ship of God's love, where Jesus is at the helm. Then you will reach the glorious goal that God has set for you. In retrospect you will see that everything that came from the Father's hand was full of eternal wisdom and conceived in His loving heart. All the time He was leading you along that particular path in order to accomplish something wonderful in your life.

Therefore, do not seek to understand God with your limited understanding. You cannot anyway, for you are a mortal being, a mere creature, limited in knowledge and reasoning. But the omnipotent, omniscient God is the everlasting One, who created heaven and earth. Instead of doubting His love and wisdom, ask yourself whether and to what extent self-will or defiance are behind your doubts and inner conflict. In reality you may be rebelling against a leading of God and unwilling to bear a cross that He has placed upon you. You evade the issue by convincing yourself that you are in inner conflict and do not know what God's will is for you. Or else you are rebellious because you do not know why God is leading you along a certain path. And all the time God is waiting for you to surrender your will fully to Him, to trust Him and persevere till He sends help or makes everything clear. So, once again, do not try to understand God. Trust Him and His love and obediently take the next step that lies before you; then your inner conflict will have to yield, and you will draw closer to God than ever before. Therefore, say ever anew:

My Father, I do not understand You,
but I trust You.

8
Personality Problems

How many sigh because of personality problems, which are often created by inherent sinful weaknesses and passions. Some are conscious of these weaknesses in their character and are distressed about them. Others suffer from the consequences. With their difficult nature and disposition they forfeit much love and sympathy in their surroundings. What a problem it is, for instance, when a person cannot manage to remain calm but flies into a rage whenever his plans are crossed or he comes under attack! It can be like an uncontrollable force operating in him, like a fire that blazes forth from his words and being. And as a result of his outbursts others are deeply wounded; they withdraw, and grow bitter towards him.

Or there is someone who is so touchy by nature that he repeatedly misinterprets factual remarks, thinking that people are getting at him, even when this is not so. He is touchy, because in his pride he cannot bear to think that others could possibly find fault with him.

Others easily grow sullen and dejected, isolating themselves at home or elsewhere. Yes, they even fall into depression and all because they resent not receiving from their fellow beings the love, honour and recognition that they long for deep down inside. Perhaps they are not even aware of this motive. All they know is that they cannot shake off their depression. They seem to be in bondage.

Still others long to live in harmony with God and their fellow beings but are unsuccessful. Dominated by a strong self-will and a spirit of rebellion, they are immediately plagued with rebellious thoughts whenever God allows troubles and difficulties to arise. Or when members of the family, people at work or anywhere else give them advice, correct them or do not do things quite the way they wanted, this immediately sparks off a rebellion, which often finds its outlet in unkind words.

If we are beset with such personality problems, others have only one comment to make about us: "That's a difficult person." In other words, it is very hard to get on with him and to put up with him. The suffering is mutual. For the person in question and for those around him. This is a suffering many have to endure, for all of us have a sinful heredity, though in some it is more noticeable than in others, be it hard-heartedness, smugness, a people-pleasing nature, coupled with the fear of offending others, or cowardice, self-indulgence, resentment, bitterness, fault-finding, criticizing, envy and jealousy — to name some examples.

Is this not a very real form of suffering? Though we may not like to admit it, we all suffer in some way because of our sinful nature, for sin is always a destructive force. It destroys peace with others, disrupts our fellowship with them, ruins something of the joy and peace in our own hearts, and spoils the joy of others. Thus a domineering and self-willed person can ruin every get-together with his desire to dominate and have his own way.

He who has eyes to see realizes what a destructive force sin is and how much suffering it causes. This is especially evident with regard to our cardinal sin, which is deeply rooted in our nature. How easy it is to feel envious and to pity ourselves when we look at others: "His character isn't marred by this sinful bondage!" Often we make it all the harder for ourselves by letting discouragement, resignation or even despair get the better of us. "How am I ever to overcome? How shall I ever become a useful member in the Body of Christ and a witness for Jesus, which is what we are supposed to be? How shall I ever endure when persecution comes upon us as Christians? Above all, how shall I ever enter the heavenly glory, the City of God, where according to Holy Scripture only those who have overcome have the right to dwell (see Revelation 3:12)?" We conclude that we are bound to our cardinal sin as if with chains of iron.

Nonetheless, it is a truth and a reality that a great treasure lies hidden even in our sinful disposition or difficult nature. All we have to do is unearth it. But we may ask, "Treasure? How can that be?" Only the sinful, only the sick, rush to the Physician of souls (see Luke 5:31f.). They alone can find the way to Him and come to know Jesus as their Saviour. They alone can experience His help and salvation. Only those who can sense how unredeemed they are need a Redeemer, and difficult people are typical examples of unredeemed people. Jesus' promise holds good for them. He has come to deliver us from our sinful bonds and make us truly free (see John 8:36). And so who will experience the saving power of Jesus the most and thus glorify Him the most? — Those who suffer the most because of their bondage to sin, for in them

Jesus can demonstrate how great His saving power is. Only His precious blood can bring about a transformation in their personalities.

This applies especially to our innate difficult disposition, which is often handed down from one generation to the next. There is a wonderful promise in the Word of God: "You know that you were ransomed from the futile ways inherited from your fathers, not with perishable things such as silver or gold, but with the precious blood of Christ, like that of a lamb without blemish or spot" (1 Peter 1:18f.). If Satan keeps trying to hold us in bondage to sin, we can oppose him with the words, "I *am* redeemed! The ransom has been paid."

Another treasure lies hidden in the sufferings of having personality problems. Keenly sensing the sinful fetters in our disposition, we are constrained to take up the battle of faith. "Fight the good fight of faith" is the Apostle Paul's summons to us (1 Timothy 6:12 AV). Only he who puts up a good fight will be crowned (see 2 Timothy 2:5). The battle of faith contains the seeds of victory. You could almost say, the very fact that we are battling makes us victors in God's eyes, such is His esteem for the battle of faith. How wonderful! But who is challenged to take up the battle? — Only he who needs to because of his difficult disposition. The harmonious types who fit in easily with others and do not cause any problems often fail to see their less overt sins, and so they do not battle against them. But the difficult person, who is troubled by his personality problems, seizes the weapon of faith and begins to wage a battle against sin and the demons in the name of Jesus and in the power of His precious blood.*

* See also Basilea Schlink, *Songs and Prayers of Victory*.

Every battle of faith counts in God's sight, even if there is little or no victory to be seen at the time. Every prayer of faith is taken into account, for the crown goes to him who keeps faith. He who battles in the power of Jesus and in union with Him cannot fail to win in the end, even if he loses many a battle because his old nature keeps asserting itself and the demons behind it refuse to yield. The final victory has been won. This is as sure as Jesus' cry of victory on the cross: "It is finished!" We are fighting under the banner of Jesus, the Victor.

What opportunities and chances are given to the person with a difficult disposition! All he needs to do is fight the battle of faith steadfastly. That means persevering in faith and not giving up. The Apostle Paul said at the end of his life, "I have kept the faith. Henceforth there is laid up for me the crown of righteousness" (2 Timothy 4:7f.). Keeping faith also applies to our personal struggle against the powers of sin and the weaknesses of our characters. And so having personality problems spurs us on to pray and battle in faith. This keeps us spiritually alive, making us constantly seek Jesus and bringing about an encounter with Him. Moreover, it honours Jesus because our honour is laid in the dust every time we are faced with our helplessness. Ever anew we are challenged to place our faith in His act of redemption, though we cannot see the victory yet. We have to look to Him for everything. Thus our plight binds us closely to Jesus, our Saviour and Redeemer. Yes, we shall draw very close to Him, our hearts filled with gratitude to have Him, for with our difficult disposition we would be lost for ever if we did not have Him. And as we experience His forgiveness ever anew, so will our love for Him grow.

Yes, having a difficult disposition makes us fight the battle of faith with all our might, for we know that only if we are faithful in this battle shall we reach the goal of glory. Therefore, let us persevere in faith and not give up. This means overcoming ourselves, for battling is painful if we are not in the mood for it and if our struggles often seem futile. But because this battle of faith contains an element of suffering, it produces something wonderful: an abundance of fruit and blessing — not only for ourselves but for others, too. Suffering is an active, creative force, always yielding fruit and blessing, provided that we accept it as coming from God and respond by saying, "Yes, Father" with a trusting heart.

So do not complain about your difficult disposition, but have faith! Take hold of the banner of faith, as it says in Psalm 20:5: "We will rejoice in thy salvation, and in the name of our God we will set up our banners" (AV). Oh, if only we would believe that Jesus looks with great love and joy upon those who steadily and devotedly battle in faith against their difficult disposition and sinful bonds day by day without growing weary. To them He can be the Saviour of sinners. To them He can reveal something of His victorious glory as the risen Lord. And thus they are a comfort to Him nowadays in view of the many people, including believers, who in spite of His act of redemption follow the dictates of their sinful desires. But those who persevere in the battle of faith He will make victors, though in His good time. Throughout our lives the Lord Jesus works at moulding us into His image. He will accomplish His objective if we do not slacken in faith but ever anew submit to His dealings and the refining process of chastenings.

God never grows weary. His love is inexhausti-
ble. Though we lose many battles in the process, if
we keep on fighting to the end, we shall one day
enter the City of God, where God will receive us
and take us into His arms. If here on earth we did
not grow weary of calling upon the name of Jesus
and claiming His victory and precious blood, in
heaven above we shall experience for ourselves:
"Victory is mine, for victory belongs to my Lord
Jesus Christ!"

9
Unanswered Prayers

Your soul is in anguish. It must be a hundred or a thousand times now that you have prayed to God in faith — for yourself, for another person, for the solution to a particular problem. But despite your fervent entreaties God's answer has not come. Why doesn't God answer? First of all we need to ask whether there is something separating us from God — a prayer hindrance that needs removing.* For instance, in a particular area of our lives we may be out of line with God's will and His command- ments. Or there may be some unforgiven sin that we have not brought to the light to be cleansed. Or perhaps we are living in irreconciliation, bitterness, resentment and envy without repenting. Holy Scripture speaks very plainly of these prayer hin- drances or prerequisites for answered prayer. If there are hindrances preventing God from hearing our prayers and we have to wait for His answer, this is meant to lead us to a wholesome repentance and a change of heart.

But even if there is no prayer hindrance, God often does not answer our prayers immediately. What could God's plan be, seeing that He has only loving intentions concerning us? In my life I have

* For further reading: Basilea Schlink, *Praying Our Way Through Life*.

experienced many answers to prayer, but time and again I had the painful experience of receiving no answer for a long while, despite my fervent entreaties. Not until ten, twenty or even thirty years later did the answer come — especially when my request was for great and decisive things in my life, our ministry or people for whom I had a particular burden. In retrospect I saw that God waits such a long time so that afterwards the wonder of receiving an answer to our prayers will be all the greater, and so, too, our joy, adoration and thanksgiving for what He has done. When fulfilment comes, it usually far exceeds our requests, for the longer and harder the time of waiting, the more abundantly God will answer our prayers, and in the end we can only stand in awe and worship. It is as if He then wishes to open the floodgates of His goodness and loving-kindness.

Waiting for the answer to our prayers holds yet another hidden blessing. God delays answering our prayers, because His plan is to grant us far more than the fulfilment of our particular request. The plus He wants to give us can only be granted if there is a prolonged waiting period. Waiting is bitter and we are not spared this painful experience, but the outcome is sweet and of lasting, eternal value.

Thus I discovered that great things were produced during such times of waiting. When God did not hear my prayers, nor seem to fulfil my requests, I repeatedly had to muster all my faith: "One day You will answer my prayers. I trust You, my Lord and my God. No prayer is in vain. You pay attention to every single one. This You promised in Your Word. And so fulfilment will come." When we have to make so many acts of faith, something wonderful happens: our crown of faith is forged in the process. What a loving plan of God! What a precious gift! Hidden from sight, important things mature during times of waiting. Battling through ever anew to a persevering faith when nothing seems to happen is a painful experience. But this suffering contains a great blessing. Having to persevere in faith ever anew makes us strong in faith, and later when faced with new trials and temptations we shall find it easier to put our trust in God and to "move mountains" by faith.

Waiting for the hour of fulfilment has yet another present in store for us: it makes us humble. In our presumptuousness we often think that God has to fulfil our requests immediately, though time and again we keep Him waiting when He has a request to make of us. But even in human relationships it is a fact: people with power and prestige can walk straight into the director's office and their requests are fulfilled right away, whereas those who are less important have to wait. Having to wait for the almighty God to answer our prayers opens our eyes to our proper place. It makes us small and humble and more like Jesus, the Son of the Most High, who said of Himself, "I am gentle and lowly in heart" (Matthew 11:29). How wonderful are God's dealings, how wise His leadings, when He does not immediately answer our prayers but lets us go through a long waiting period! In this way we shall be graced with the humility that adorns a child of God, the humility to submit ourselves to God and His incomprehensible sovereign rule when our prayers seem to go unheeded. God in His love has a plan in leading us along paths where we have to wait and wait again. Faith, patience and humility are being wrought in us in the process.

In the end we shall see that the Lord did hear our prayers and fulfil our requests, provided that these were not conceived in self-will or disobedience but in accordance with Jesus' will. After the long waiting period we shall then receive with humble hearts what we asked for. Filled with gratitude to God, our Father, we shall never forget what He has done for us. Our adoration will be all the more fervent, since it will come from a humble heart, and we shall treat with reverence and special care that which we received from Him. We shall have drawn closer to God and come to know His all-loving heart, which can never disappoint us, but in wise and fatherly love brings us up.

It is up to us whether or not we make the most of such waiting periods, allowing the Lord to do His great work of transforming us into His image, so that one day we shall be with Him and behold Him face to face for all eternity — a joy granted only to those who have become Christ-like.

However, even after a prolonged period of waiting, the Lord does not always grant us a direct answer to our prayers. Sometimes He not only lets us wait so long because it is for our good, but answers our prayers in a completely different way than we had wished or imagined. For instance, we may pray that God will change the attitude of those who make life hard for us or even hate us. Yet our request is not granted. Why not? Again, Jesus in His wisdom intends to transform us into His image, the image of the Lamb, so that we shall love our adversaries and bless them. With this attitude of merciful love towards our enemies we can be a blessing for those who oppose Jesus and sometimes we may even be able to overcome them. And so the Lord did hear our prayer after all, but not the way we thought He would.

One thing is sure. God always answers our prayers, though sometimes in a way that we do not understand Him at first, for His thoughts, plans and purposes are much greater than our thoughts — and far more wonderful! He loves us beyond man's telling and wants to bless us far more than we could ever imagine or expect. In over sixty years of following the Lord this has always been my experience whenever my prayers did not seem to be answered. So let us trust implicitly in the love of God, for the word of Scripture holds true: "Ask, and it will be given you."

10
Untalented

You lack talent. You feel inadequate to handle certain jobs and accomplish certain tasks, which others manage with effortless ease. Perhaps you are handicapped by some physical defect — lack of strength, delicate health, or old age. You do not easily win the affection and esteem of others, because you do not have an attractive appearance or an outgoing personality. You suffer greatly, for you feel at a disadvantage and neglected by God. The talented person tackles everything efficiently and successfully; he is quick to take in the situation; he is discerning and has a good memory; he has a say in everything because of his extensive knowledge — and knowledge means power. But you feel more or less ignored. He who has a charming personality is popular with others and immediately makes friends, whereas you are given the cold shoulder; no one takes an interest in you.

Finding yourself in a situation like this, you may ask, "What will help me to bear this suffering? What can I do so that it doesn't get me down or make me unhappy?" There is something that can help. It helped me when I had to suffer because of my inadequacy in one particular area of my life — the inability to communicate in English. During many trips abroad I was painfully aware of this deficiency. For my ministry it was essential to understand English and speak the language, but I was unable to, not having a flair for languages and having primarily studied French and the classical languages at school. When later the Lord did not give me any more time or the opportunity to overcome this deficiency, I wrote down the following prayer:

O Father, I am willing to be poor,
inadequate, helpless. And with this Yes
I want to honour You.
Then You will accomplish what I cannot do,
and in spite of everything You, and You alone,
will pave the way for Your message.

This act of dedication transformed that which I found so hard to bear. I discovered that when you abandon your wishes and will unreservedly to God you become one with Him, and this oneness fills the heart with peace.

True, I was handicapped by this deficiency. The price of suffering had to be paid. Due to the poor translation of my talks I was unable to convey properly the message entrusted to me, although I had undertaken these long journeys expressly for this purpose. Not knowing the language well enough, I tended to be left out during important conversations and interviews and could not reach the hearts of others as I would have liked to. But in all this the Lord would grant me a deep inner joy and I would thank Him for making me small and helpless, because I knew that He loves the small and helpless and would carry out my ministry some other way. Time and again I experienced how wonderfully He can do this. Years later, for instance, the Lord gave us a film and video ministry for spreading His

Word, and with His help I was able to deliver messages in English after all, which were then televised to millions in the English-speaking world.

And so I would like to encourage you to say, "Yes, Father" in view of your particular inadequacy, inability, deficiency. It comes from God your Father, who has hidden within it a great blessing that others richly endowed with gifts and external advantages could envy you. Because of your helplessness, you will draw close to your Lord Jesus, the humbled Son of God — closer than perhaps anyone else. Poor — but rich, because you are committed to His will — you have the approval of the Father resting upon you.

God has yet another present in store for the poor, inadequate and untalented. Not being richly endowed with talents makes you humble. Those who are highly gifted are in danger of becoming over-confident and proud, and they will painfully experience that God resists the proud. But to whom does God give grace? — The humble. If God has denied you some talent and you give Him a wholehearted Yes, humbly accepting this as coming from His fatherly hand, you are under His grace. And if every time you feel inadequate, you approach the Father as a child of His, asking for help, you are actually richly blessed, whereas the naturally gifted person who does not use his many gifts in dependence upon God is, in fact, the poor one.

So remember, having a reputation for competence, possessing various abilities and advantages, and being good at certain things are not decisive. What matters is not the way others regard me but how God regards me. This is of everlasting importance, as will be evident in the life to come. Conversely, the good opinion that others may have of me applies only to the short span of my earthly life and is of value only to mortal man, who is a mere nothing in the eyes of God. Consider what the Bible says. Those who are worth nothing in the eyes of the world — the poor, the untalented, the insignificant — are worth a lot to God (see 1 Corinthians 1:27f.). "Man looks on the outward appearance, but the Lord looks on the heart" (1 Samuel 16:7).

So begin now and rejoice in your nothingness: "I am worth a lot to God. He gives me His special love, for every child of His lacking gifts and cleverness has a special place in His heart. He can glorify Himself far more in the life of an untalented person like me than in the life of someone wise and clever!" If you rejoice like this in your inability and give thanks that in your poverty you are rich in God, your inferiority complex will disappear and you will no longer feel unhappy. For you know that you are accepted by God, that He loves you and has a special regard for you — He who is the Maker and Father of us all, our Judge, whose judgment alone counts.

There is something else that will comfort you. Your inadequacy and lack of ability in certain respects give you an advantage. Because of your helplessness reliance upon God comes naturally to you. Ever anew you have to ask Him to come to your aid, since you are unable to manage by yourself. This deepens your dependence upon Him and leads you into a close relationship with your God and Father, far more so than the person who can manage everything "by himself". In God you will find a rich source of joy and love, which flows from

Him to you. This love, in turn, will kindle you with love for your fellow beings — and what a precious thing that is, for love is the greatest of all gifts (see 1 Corinthians 13)! Love for your fellow beings will then make them open their hearts to you, so that you will find even greater receptiveness than if you had many talents and other advantages. So love — and your sadness and inhibitions because of your inadequacy will disappear. The love of Jesus will have triumphed in you.

11
Growing Old

Whenever I visited an old relative of mine and asked him how he was faring, his reply echoed the trials of growing old: "Ah, everything's deteriorating. My sight, my hearing, everything's going."

How hard it is when our powers of comprehension decline! This gentleman, a clever man who had a prominent part in intellectual circles, did not even read the newspapers now; nor was he any longer able to follow current events; nor did he read books; for he could no longer take in everything properly. What a humiliation! He still wanted to understand and could not.

Then came the lament, "My memory is failing!" Till his eighties this gentleman was blessed with an excellent memory. But then his capacity to remember dwindled and he could no longer express his views as he would have liked to, for the facts had slipped his memory. Thus when various topics were raised, he was unable to join in the conversation, being now ignorant of these matters.

All his movements, particularly when walking, used to be brisk. But now he could only move forward with difficulty, leaning on someone's arm or with the aid of a walking stick. He was dependent upon various props. Now he constantly needed help. In every respect he experienced the wretchedness of our human existence when God takes away physical and mental faculties and makes us poor in the truest sense of the word and therefore dependent upon others.

Many old people also suffer emotionally. Often they are all alone. Their marriage partner may have died. Their children are grown up and live elsewhere with their families. Many of their friends and acquaintances have already died. And who really takes an interest in an old person? Very few old people receive love — especially if they did not sow much love during their lives.

Yes, growing old is a form of suffering. Moreover, it is often accompanied by various illnesses that naturally come with old age. The inability to cope as one would like to faces the old person everywhere. This is a potential danger. He may rebel in his heart against his condition and even grow bitter, thus making life harder for himself and unbearable for those around him. As the saying goes, "Growing old is an art that not everyone can master."

Yet not only can the art of growing old be mastered, but a special radiance can rest upon an old person. God wants to transform this suffering into blessing, yes, glory. This old relative of mine was a testimony of this. Having much time for quiet and prayer because of his diminishing mental faculties and his physical condition, he would time and again consider his life in the sight of God. Then, to my astonishment, whenever I came to visit him, I heard how the Lord had shown him something else that had been amiss in his life. For instance, he would say that his many abilities had made him proud and ambitious, and so he was grateful that he still had time to repent of this. When the Lord now led him along paths that would make him small and humble, he wanted to accept this gladly − in thanksgiving to God.

A transformation took place in him as he accepted the truth about himself. He humbled himself under the mighty hand of God and was filled with repentance for everything that had not been good in the past. How different his life was now! Once he used to be a prominent and much-loved man in a position of leadership. But now that God took away everything from him and he became dependent upon others he became more and more humble, grateful for the smallest service rendered to him.

Now that his mental faculties were diminishing, his spiritual faculties grew from year to year. It was remarkable. When he prayed it was as if he suddenly had the best memory of all. He brought before the Lord all the needs of those for whom he had a burden as well as the concerns and problems of various Christian organizations.

Yes, when the outward man with all his gifts and abilities wastes away, the inward man can be progressively renewed (see 2 Corinthians 4:16). In the same measure that the gifts pertaining to human, earthly life are diminished, in that measure the spiritual gifts will emerge and gain in strength. But there is a prerequisite for this: faith in our Lord Jesus Christ. He who believes in Him has eternal life, which is divine life − and divine life is immortal. This truth is demonstrated in people in whom Jesus Christ lives, for He is the Eternal One, whose divine strength can never be diminished or killed. Though everything we may possess in the way of human strength and gifts gradually wastes away, if

Christ dwells in us He will manifest Himself all the more in His strength and glory.

What a blessing there is in growing old! What an opportunity for the glory of God to shine forth! Thus this old gentleman became a focus of spiritual life for many. They came to ask for his prayers or his blessing. By no means was he unwanted, without a task or purpose in life, just a burden to everyone else, as is often said of old people. Rather, he had a great ministry, which brought much blessing to others, for Jesus Christ was alive in him. Because the trials of old age made him humble and small, Jesus was able to gain more and more room in him and shine forth from him all the mightier. And since this man went over his whole life in repentance, Christ could glorify Himself to an ever greater extent through him and grant him spiritual power.

God wants springs of everlasting joy to well up in old age. Yes, old age can bring real joy with it, since all those who love our Lord Jesus will — as they grow older — be characterized by the joy of soon going home to the One they love. "Soon I shall see Him. Soon I shall be in my eternal home, in the kingdom of peace, love and everlasting joy, in the City of God, where I shall dwell in bliss." God wants to impart this joy to those who undergo the trials of old age in union with Him, as we saw in the case of that old gentleman.

One thing we should not do: rebel in our hearts against the sufferings of growing old. In so doing we kill the divine, eternal life within us. For every rebelliousness separates us from God and prevents Him from pouring His divine life into us.

However, those who accept the trials of growing

old and fully surrender their wills to our Lord Jesus Christ will experience the reality of that great promise of His: "My grace is sufficient for you, for my power is made perfect in weakness" (2 Corinthians 12:9). And what is this power? — The power of love, joy, prayer and authority in the Lord. All this is to become ours in our old age. A wonderful prospect as we grow older.

Oh, if only everyone who has not yet fully surrendered his life to Jesus in all that he is and has would now commit himself to Him and love Him above all else! It's worth it! Joy and happiness dwell in those in whom Jesus Christ has made His abode. This is especially visible in old people. They reflect Him, bring joy to others and live in blissful expectation of the day when the Lord will call them home. Yes, in Jesus Christ they have everything they need and desire. For when we come to nought, He who is all in all, can do all things in us and give us everything we lack. And, above, we shall shine like the stars in His kingdom.

12
Want and Need

Gone are the days of affluence — for the western nations, too. Economic crises are spreading throughout the world and are threatening to develop into a worldwide economic disaster with dire poverty and famine in its wake. One firm after the other is going bankrupt; prices are constantly rising, while unemployment prevails. You may be painfully aware that you are growing poorer. The little money you possess is losing in value. With poverty gnawing at your heart, you wonder how you are going to make both ends meet for your family.

The concern that poverty will soon enter your home or has already moved in is a form of suffering. But God can transform this suffering, too, into gain for you. He can see to it that in spite of everything your basic needs are supplied and, most important of all, that you experience Him as never before. When will that happen? — When you come to the Lord with your cares and wants. So long as you had everything in abundance, you may have taken His gifts for granted and did not make a point of talking with your heavenly Father about your daily needs. But start calling upon Him now for help. Trust Him. He knows what you need and can make the poor rich. The heavenly Father has compassion on the needy and will come to their aid.

This we experienced in the aftermath of World War II when streams of refugees crossed our country without any belongings, having lost during the flight the little they could take with them. They were poor in every respect. Even those who used to be wealthy landowners possessed nothing now. Yet what did many testify a number of years later when they had re-established themselves and were well-provided for? "We were much happier while we were poor. We were constantly driven to call upon the Lord and trust in His help, and then we experienced miraculous instances of His provision. From various quarters we would unexpectedly receive things we needed, although from the human point of view it was well-nigh impossible. In a personal way we tasted the love of the heavenly Father ever anew. What a deeply happy relationship we had with Him! And how close He was to us! At every instance of help, at every token of His love, we were gripped with a joy that we have never known since then. We often long for those days again!"

Yes, it is true. He makes the poor rich. His heart goes out to them. We, too, experienced this in our Sisterhood, which was founded just after World War II. In those days food was very scarce, and when a number of Sisters came to join our household, none of them could bring with them their allotted hundredweight of potatoes, which every person had been rationed for the winter. What were we to live on? Potatoes were our staple diet and we had only enough for two. Quite apart from that, we lacked other food supplies, money, clothing articles, household goods, and so on. But then we experienced miracle upon miracle. For instance, God multiplied our potatoes after I prayed with the Kitchen Sister every evening in the cellar, where the few potatoes were stored, and asked the Lord to bless them. We had enough to eat the whole year, although there were seven more of us as well as guests. It also so happened that the missing household utensils including a prayed-for broom, in those days a rarity, would suddenly arrive. What rejoicing there was when a package came with a broom! The donor had added a note that the Lord had put it in her heart to send us a broom.

I could continue like this for many pages. Yes, we have experienced for over 35 years that God keeps His word. If we seek first the Kingdom of God, that is, if we dedicate ourselves, our efforts and every donation for the extension of His kingdom, if we live according to His commandments and in contrition and repentance, then all the other things we need to exist will be "added unto" us (Matthew 6:33 AV). Living by faith, we did not receive a regular income, nor charge anything for our services. We were poor. What were we to live on in the initial years? At that time we did not have a proper circle of friends. Yet all our needs were supplied. We always found the table spread before us.* To this day we live from the miraculous provision of God and experience the reality of Jesus' words: in God's eyes we are worth more than the lilies of the field, which He clothes so beautifully. Now we are approximately 200 Sisters. The donations we receive from our circle of friends are used

* For further reading: Basilea Schlink, *Realities — The Miracles of God Experienced Today* (American title: *Realities of Faith*).

for the work in the Kingdom of God and yet we still sit at a laid table and have everything we need for living.

However, on the path of poverty we have discovered ever anew that if we are lacking something, our needs will not be met automatically in answer to prayer. As mentioned in an earlier chapter, our prayers have power with God and His promise holds good only if we remove all prayer hindrances, such as any tension or irreconciliation among us, bitterness in our hearts, or any other failure to take the commandments of God seriously enough. It means confessing our sins in contrition, asking forgiveness of Jesus and our fellow-men and turning over a new leaf. According to Scripture this is the condition for answered prayer and only on this condition can we experience anew that God hears the pleas of the poor, as it says in His Word: "He delivers the needy when he calls, the poor and him who has no helper" (Psalm 72:12).

Thus it can be a joy to be poor, for poverty contains a wonderful treasure like every other suffering that we bear with Jesus: an abundance of joy and glory. And if in our poverty we are willing to share with the needy the little we have, God will keep His word: "Give, and it will be given to you" (Luke 6:38). Those who are poor because they readily give of what they have will be the richest of all, for God will repay them abundantly. A missionary who had been kidnapped by guerrillas and spent many weeks trekking through the bush told us the following story. When one of the guards asked her to give him her medicine, she gave it to him, but with a heavy heart, for it meant so much to her; without it she would never be able to bear the strain of those gruelling weeks. Then God worked a miracle, and the opposite happened of what was to be expected. Her health was better than when she had the medicine.

We should expect similar acts of divine intervention when we find ourselves in situations of need. How soon can a worldwide economic crisis lead to a time of famine! If we then give away our last piece of bread, God will make us rich in our poverty, strengthen and sustain us, for the sense of His presence transforms everything, overruling the very laws of nature.

So let us not fear times of privation and famine. Rather, let us fear God, not taking sin lightly but following paths that are pleasing to Him. Let us live according to His commandments and for the extension of His kingdom and gladly give of what we have. Then as the poor and needy we shall be the richest of all — through Him and in Him.

13
Fear of Death

How often you hear it said nowadays: "The diagnosis is cancer. The patient probably doesn't have long to live." Or you have reached the age when you will inevitably meet with death soon. Every day death takes its toll on the streets, with thousands of fatal traffic casualties yearly. Who can know whether his next drive will be his last? Violence and murder are on the increase. Uprisings make life insecure. War is an ever-present threat. Death is lurking on all sides, and you are gripped by fear of death.

Fear of death must be a special kind of fear, indeed, the greatest fear of all. Otherwise the expression "he's scared to death" would not be used so commonly to describe a person tormented by fear. Jesus knew the full implications of death. "Moved with indignation and deeply troubled," He came to the mourning sisters after the death of Lazarus. And on the way to the tomb He wept (John 11:33-38 LB). In the Garden of Gethsemane when He wrestled with death — the prince of death, in fact, — He shed tears and sweated drops of blood. So great was His agony that His face mirrored horror and deepest distress when He went to His disciples.

Not without reason did our forefathers write on the walls of their houses and in their accounting books, "Memento mori" — "Remember that thou must die." Death is the most crucial event in our lives because of its finality. Why do we fear death? It is not just the fact that death removes us from this life; it is the fear and uncertainty of what lies beyond — this is what often torments us. "Where shall I awake? Where shall I find myself then?" We know that what we sow in this life will yield a harvest, depending on the seeds we have sown. At death we have to enter another world and appear before Him who is the Judge of the living and the dead. Paul was also referring to believers when he wrote, "All of us must appear before Christ, to be judged by him. Each one will receive what he deserves, according to everything he has done, good or bad, in his bodily life" (2 Corinthians 5:10 GNB). Death inevitably brings us to the place where we shall be called to account for our actions and our whole life — something that we may have wished to avoid at all costs during our earthly existence.

In the face of death we no longer have control over anything or can decide what is to be done. We are entirely in God's hands. Most people, even those who are godless, are overcome with mortal fear before their death. Having to walk through the valley of the shadow of death is probably the greatest suffering that we have to endure. With the approach of death we are faced with the question, "Will Satan have a right to us and take us to be with him in his kingdom for ever?" Satan is the accuser. Every unconfessed and unrepented sin in our lives gives him a right to us. This is why many people, perhaps including you, are gripped with fear at the prospect of dying.

Merely to dismiss the thought of death is not the way to overcome your fear of death. The only thing that can help you is to prepare for death. Remember that your last hour is coming, the hour when your fate will be decided. Either you will be carried off as Satan's prey to his kingdom of darkness. Or you will be privileged to enter the heavenly dwelling-place that Jesus has prepared for us (see John 14:2). However, not even for believers is this a matter of course, for Satan has a right to us if we criticize others, if we live in strife, bitterness, resentment and irreconciliation, even giving room to hatred in our hearts. The Bible is speaking of believers when it says that those who do such things shall not enter the kingdom of God (see Galatians 5:19-21). Therefore, prepare yourself, so that in the hour of death you will be carried by the angels into Jesus' kingdom. This will be granted to you if you did not persist in the sins of the world or the more subtle sins of pharisaism and hypocrisy, but came to the cross of Jesus in contrition every time you sinned in thought, word or deed, confessing your sins before God and man and asking forgiveness and living in reconciliation with others. God is gracious to sinners who repent. He permits them to enter His kingdom when their last moment has come.

How urgent is Jesus' appeal to us while we are on earth and while there is still a time of grace: "Repent of your sins, confess them!" Pray ever anew for light so that they will be shown to you and you can bring them to Jesus. Then you will experience something wonderful: the forgiveness of your sins. The blood of Jesus will cover your guilt, and the gateway to paradise will be opened to you as it was for the penitent thief on the cross, who acknowledged his guilt. Believe that your fear of death will

71

yield when you have acknowledged your sins and received forgiveness. Then you will have peace, great peace, now and even more so later when you pass through the valley of death to be with your heavenly Father for ever.

So listen to the voice of Jesus calling to you today: "Come to Me. Repent now while there is still time. Come, so that you may receive forgiveness. Then Satan will lose his right to you, and instead of death bringing damnation for you, you shall be pardoned." Even so, we must all appear before the judgment seat of Christ. No one is spared this. But this judgment will not concern salvation. Reward or loss of reward will be the issue, for we shall be rewarded according to the fruit we have borne in our earthly lives.

The agony of having to face death and walk through the dark valley of death can be turned into joy, yes, everlasting joy and glory. But for whom? — For him who has prepared himself beforehand, allowing the light of God to fall upon his life and convict him of sin. So humble yourself now before God and man. Follow now in Jesus' footsteps, love Him above all else — love for Jesus always includes love for our neighbour — and give Him your all. Then you will experience that not only does death lose its terrors, but something wonderful happens, as many believers have experienced. The closer they came to death, the closer heaven was. They were immersed in streams of divine joy and bliss. Yes, Jesus drew so close to them with His angels and saints that these dying believers rejoiced in their hearts with one great longing: soon to be home with the One they loved.

Never shall I forget how it was with our Sister

Claudia. Only 35 years old, bubbling over with life, never sick, filled with a contagious joy and a fervent love for Jesus, she was suddenly afflicted with a severe blood disease during her ministry in Italy. She returned to the Mother House and was then sent to a specialist clinic. A few days later we heard that there was nothing more the doctors could do for Sister Claudia. Her days were numbered. We were filled with apprehension at having to break the news to her. But what did Mother Martyria and I experience when we entered her sickroom? (Actually, she already knew, especially after a hint from the doctor.) She looked up at us with a radiant smile that was not of this world. The Lord Jesus had come to greet her, and the glory of heaven rested on her features. It had happened during her return trip from Rome, as she recorded in her diary:

> The plane flew towards the sun. All at once it seemed to me as though the Lord Jesus were asking me, "And if this illness should lead to death?" O Jesus, in this moment You have filled my heart with such infinite longing that I can scarcely restrain the surging joy, soon, soon to see You, soon, soon to embrace You! Will this flight home be a flight into the arms of my Lord? Will it be the bridal flight for me?*

Jesus has conquered the power of death, and if we believe in Him, we shall experience His victory and the grace that He has won for us. Not only will death lose its terrors, but — like Stephen (see Acts

* See Basilea Schlink, *If I Only Love Jesus, The Story of Sister Claudia.*

7:54ff.) – in dying we shall see the glory of God. This will be the experience of those who "lived in heaven" while on earth. Because they were united in love with Jesus, their innermost being was with Jesus who, seated at the right hand of God, is the very centre of heaven. Death is the gateway to divine life, to the kingdom of glory, for those who lived solely for Jesus, spent themselves for Him and followed His path of lowliness and obedience, surrendering their wills to Him and trusting Him. Yes, if for them living meant Christ, then dying will be gain for them (see Philippians 1:21). The divine life in their hearts cannot die in the hour of death. Rather this divine life will be manifest in all its fullness when they go home to the One they loved above all else, Jesus Christ, whom they shall behold in eternity.

It is incomprehensible that the suffering caused by fear of death can be changed into the most blissful and heavenly joy. What a wonderful God we have! What miracles He works, transforming deepest suffering into supreme joy! Death brings us home to God and His kingdom of everlasting happiness.

14
Unfair Treatment

You ask, "What shall I do? The way others at home or at work take unfair advantage of me! I can hardly bear it. They expect me to go on working while they take their ease. They leave me to do all the unpleasant tasks. They don't care how much this costs me in the way of extra time, energy, and so on. Life with my colleagues and family has become a real burden for me." You refuse to be treated as a doormat that others walk over. Besides, it goes against your sense of justice.

Yes, unfair treatment can be a painful form of suffering. Often it causes us much damage in our careers as well as a loss of money and goods. Above all, there is a great danger that we shall grow resentful and bitter. Perhaps we have taken great pains to build up a small business when someone comes along and borrows a sum of money without repaying it. He may even grow annoyed with us and speak ill of us. And so we have to suffer doubly. It is not easy to see hard-earned money being squandered by others.

How are we to cope with this suffering? I once experienced in a small measure what it is like to be taken advantage of. Later I was to experience this on a larger scale, not that there is anything unusual about it, for it is part of the normal Christian life. My first encounter with this was about 35 years ago. In our Sisterhood of Mary we had just published the first booklets containing the message entrusted to us by God. It was a great venture of faith to get together the necessary funds for the printing costs in those days of dire poverty, and we were filled with gratitude when the bills could actually be paid. In the small room that served as an exhibition for hand-written cards and other artistic products of our workshop, we then displayed the booklets in small piles. And what happened?

An itinerant Christian bookseller who toured the villages, going from house to house to offer Christian literature, called on us one day. In our exhibition room his companion explained to him, "You can take what you want. It's all free of charge." Thereupon this man filled a suitcase with our literature and left without dropping a coin in the box for free-will offerings. Our literature and products had no fixed price, for as a faith ministry we leave it to the individual how much he wishes to contribute by way of donation. Taking advantage of this opportunity, this man then went and sold the books. I was troubled about this and could feel displeasure welling up in my heart towards him because of the way he had treated us and the methods he used in carrying out his literature ministry.

But then I realized that God Himself had sent us this man. He was to be the instrument that God would use to work on me. This incident had taken me by surprise and, at first, I had not trusted in God enough. Now I was to learn to rely on God and to reckon with His help, which we can experience only if we follow Jesus along His pathway, the way of the Lamb. In years to come more serious incidents followed and the full implications of the way of the Lamb became increasingly clear to me. Like a lamb Jesus bore injustice during His earthly life, though He was the Son of God. He surrendered His right to God the Father, who judges righteously and who in His good time would vindicate the Son's cause (see Psalm 9:4). For us treading the way of the Lamb means instead of inwardly asserting our rights and growing annoyed with the person who takes advantage of us and does wrong to us, we patiently accept this suffering as coming from God's hand and then commit the whole situation to Him, trusting that He will care for us and contend for us.

Treading the way of the Lamb does not always mean that we should put up with everything. There may also be situations when we are obliged to help our neighbour to see where he has erred. But this should be done in a humble, loving and forgiving spirit. In any event, treading the way of the Lamb means loving, blessing and doing good to the person who takes unfair advantage of us. Then God will also bless and help us. As I increasingly learnt to tread the way of the Lamb and to bear injustice and unfairness quietly and with thoughts of blessing towards the other person, my trust grew in God's ability to more than compensate for all the damage done.

As I thought of our Lord Jesus, this pathway became very precious to me. It was not just that I did not have to strive for my rights. Now I discovered that behind it all was a wonderful plan of God to draw me closer to Himself. For on the way of the Lamb I was deeply united with Him. Nor was that all. Whenever others wronged me and took unfair advantage of me, this gave my heavenly Father the opportunity of caring for me and demonstrating, in His good time, His power and aid.

This I was to experience abundantly in the subsequent history of our Sisterhood. You could say that to the extent we gave up our rights and thus, humanly speaking, put the continuation of our ministry at risk, to that extent did the Lord intervene on our behalf and supply all our needs without our making any appeals for funds. At our retreat centre, in our small nursing home, at our book displays, in whatever services rendered, it was left entirely to the people as to whether and how much they wished to contribute by donation. Of course, a risk was involved, for they could have taken unfair advantage of us. However, we have never suffered any lack and to this day we have been able to carry out our worldwide ministries without ever incurring debts. A professor of mathematics once called this "heavenly mathematics".

Are we willing to let others take unfair advantage of us for once? God our Father is waiting for our readiness, because then He can enrich our lives, above all, spiritually, by drawing us closer to Himself as we learn to trust in Him. We shall experience what a blissful thing it is to be a child of His. Instead of having to be dependent upon others, we can tell Him everything and receive from Him all that we need. And if He then allows us to suffer injustice, His objective is to remould us into the image of the Lamb. We shall draw close to our Lord Jesus, becoming one with Him, our long-suffering Lord, who bore so much injustice. Thus from this suffering, too, rivers of blessing flow forth. It is not when we demand our rights but when we follow this path that such blissful and intimate communion with Jesus is ours. The way of the Lamb, which unites us with Jesus and fosters a childlike relationship of trust with the heavenly Father, leads to the City of God, where we shall be with Him forever. And so what does this suffering bring us? Joy and bliss for all eternity. Believe this.

15
Facing Hatred and Slander

Everyone who has ever been hated or slandered by
a person or a whole group and whose name has
been dragged through the mud, knows what
wounds this inflicts upon the soul. We say that
hatred kills. Yes, hatred is psychological murder.
Slander and lies can have a devastating effect on a
person, making him run down and ill. They can
damage many things in his life — his prestige, his
reputation and career.

The source of hatred is very often envy or
jealousy. If a person is filled with hatred towards
someone, it makes no difference if his assertions
are proven to be slanderous statements and lies.
Nothing will convince him of his error. On the contrary, when he is confronted with the truth, his
hatred becomes even greater.

We may ask how we are to endure all this. Expo-
sure to hatred, slander, shame and disgrace — even
if it is for Jesus' sake — is surely one of the greatest
forms of suffering. There are people who may be
able to endure many kinds of suffering bravely, but
when disgrace comes into their lives, they are unable to bear it. And yet Jesus pronounced the
longest beatitude over those whose names are cast
out as evil and who are reviled and lied about on
His account. Jesus challenges us to "rejoice in that
day, and leap for joy, for behold, your reward is

great in heaven" (Luke 6:22f.; cf. Matthew 5:11f.).

But how does this joy become ours? We wish we had it, but usually our hearts are deeply wounded when we encounter hatred and disgrace. We either give up or else we become embittered. Rebellious-ness or even hatred surge up within us when we think of the person who has wounded us and done us wrong. The lies go against our sense of justice; our indignation is roused. Even at night we may have no peace, because we are plagued by bitter thoughts and accusations. All too easily we lapse into rebellion against God, too, complaining to Him, "Why do You send all this disgrace into my life? Why do You allow my reputation to be ruined? Why do I have to suffer so much hatred?" We think that this wound in our hearts will never heal; it is so deep.

From personal experience I know how wounds of disgrace can burn. This began years ago when a revival broke out in our youth work, leading to the founding of our Sisterhood. When later our little Land of Canaan was established and gained signifi-cance, becoming a spiritual centre with visitors from all over the world, more and more people be-came envious. The slander and hatred grew at the same rate. Not only did I receive letters filled with lies and accusations and ascribing evil things to me, but some personages launched a real campaign against our Sisterhood and in particular against my person. Letters were sent to many Christian or-ganizations, warning them against us and threatening them with countermeasures if they still maintained contact with us and passed on my literature. Believers were urged to burn my writ-ings, and in many cases these instructions were obeyed. Warnings were issued against me at public meetings and on tapes, thus spreading the slander throughout the country. Our adversaries went so far as to maintain that I and our organization were demonic because we have the gifts of the Spirit, lead a life of repentance and prayer, and trust God for all our needs. This was described as something contrary to the teaching of Holy Scripture. One publication after the other was released containing libel against us. These were passed on in circles of committed Christians and even reached mission stations in distant lands. Usually they were accepted as the truth, for it was considered impossible that believers could lie.

When you are wounded so deeply, how do you bear the pain? How do you overcome? God showed me a way. He first helped me to realize that ultimately all this did not come from people but from Him. I had to learn both the necessity and privilege of saying, "It is the Lord!" Whatever He does comes from His loving heart and is in accordance with an eternal, loving and wise plan. It is meant to serve to our highest good and bring us a blessing. A treasure lies hidden in this suffering, which is meant to make us more like Jesus. If we believe this, peace and serenity will enter our hearts. And so I was able to say ever anew, "Yes, Father, it comes from Your hands, and so I will accept it."

Our Lord Jesus Christ Himself has trodden this path. He was disgraced, slandered, dishonoured, laden with false accusations, and finally nailed to the cross as a criminal — He, the pure and holy One. And I was His disciple. I belonged to Him. Now I had the privilege of standing at His side in truth and experiencing, in some measure, the fel-

lowship of His sufferings — a special grace. Did not
Jesus say, "If they persecuted me, they will perse-
cute you" (John 15:20)? This meant that I was on the
right track as a disciple of Jesus. For it is also written, "A student is not greater than his teacher. A
servant is not above his master. The student shares
his teacher's fate. The servant shares his master's!
And since I, the master of the household, have
been called 'Satan,' how much more will you!"
(Matthew 10:24f. LB). Now I became more deeply
united with Jesus. Now I was privileged to apply
the Bible verse to myself: "If you are reproached for
the name of Christ, blessed are you, for the Spirit of
glory and of God rests upon you. On their part he is
blasphemed, but on your part he is glorified" (1
Peter 4:14 RAV). What a precious gift that is! My
heart was comforted, and I consecrated myself
anew to my disgraced and blasphemed Lord, with
the deep desire to share His path.

The Lord also showed me that this pathway of
disgrace was part of His plan to refine me. He
wanted to grant me a deeper release from those
typically human reactions: asserting one's rights
instead of showing a merciful love towards one's
enemies. Along this path of chastening God
wanted to work in me so that more and more of this
merciful love could be found in my life. He had a
wonderful and holy purpose in allowing my adversaries to wound me. Merciful love was to flow forth
from these wounds. To this end Jesus redeemed us
when He hung on the cross, slandered, hated and
filled with suffering. From His wounded heart
flowed nothing but merciful, forgiving love towards those who had hated and slandered Him
and caused Him to die on the cross.

This is what Jesus wanted to achieve in me, and He wants to do the same for you when He leads you into situations when you experience disgrace and suffer injustice. He wants to evoke in us the most beautiful thing of all: a merciful love towards our enemies, towards those who not only hurt us but perhaps even hate and slander us. From our wounds there should flow forth love and forgiveness instead of bitterness.

I was incapable of producing this love for my adversaries by my own efforts, since I was still concerned with my justification when I thought of those who wronged me — even though I endured everything silently, without a word in defence. But Jesus, the Lamb of God, went for us the way of the Lamb. He was crucified as a lamb and accomplished His act of salvation, so that from His wounds salvation and redemption would flow forth. His holy blood has the redemptive power to change us into loving, merciful persons. Thus ever anew I claimed the blood of the Lamb, that He might make of me a little lamb and that I might learn not only to bear injustice but to love with all my heart. Jesus heard my prayer, and with the passing of time He granted me an ever-increasing measure of merciful love for my adversaries.

Whoever longs, as I did, to love his enemies with a merciful love can claim the blood of Jesus. Jesus' saving act is valid. We have been redeemed so that we might love. And Jesus' redemption will take effect in our lives if we humbly admit our failure to live up to Jesus' commandment to love our enemies, and if we are now willing to suffer their blows. Then in the power of His redemption we shall even consider it a privilege to love our enemies. I experienced that an ever deeper peace filled my heart in the process and then I also tasted the joy that Jesus describes in the Sermon on the Mount.

The joy that He gives us begins even while we are in suffering and it directs our gaze towards heaven. Above, we shall have no more enemies. We shall no longer be hated, persecuted, disgraced and slandered. No more lies will be spread about us. Rather we shall have fellowship with those who love and we shall dwell with the Lord Jesus, who is Love eternal. This thought was and still is a great comfort for me. We may joyfully look forward to the day when we go home to the Lord. In heaven crowns will be given to those who overcame here below and who responded to hatred with love. True to His word, Jesus will grant an abundance of joy and glory in His kingdom for all eternity to those who suffered hatred and slander for His name's sake.

Yes, the sufferings of this present time are transient, and so, too, are the disgrace, hatred, degradation and slander and everything else we have to endure here. In contrast, that which we shall find in eternity is lasting. And in eternity — as Holy Scripture says — those who were degraded, hated and slandered here will be highly honoured. But even in this life untold blessings await us. In the midst of hatred and slander we can learn to love our enemies — indeed, nowhere does this love thrive so well as on this soil! Being able to love enriches our lives and makes us far happier than if we had never experienced the hatred of others.

Facing hatred and slander is a particularly severe form of suffering. But for this very reason a special

blessing lies hidden within it. Believe this! Disgrace
is intended to make us smaller and humbler. And is
this not what we long for? Do we not yearn to become like Jesus, so that one day we may behold
Him face to face? When pierced by the arrows of
hatred and slander, let us submit ourselves to the
Lord ever anew with a Yes and declare, "O my Lord
Jesus, O my Father, I want to undergo this suffering, for I want to share Your path. I need this particular suffering, for disgrace is humbling and it
will make me humbler." Suffering will lose its sting
when we make an act of dedication like this. To me
it was as if Jesus were saying then, "Bow down
deeper and deeper. Then My grace will come upon
you, and you will draw close to Me, your degraded
Lord, who chose to follow this path of untold scorn
and shame." And what greater joy could there be
than being close to Him?

Appendix

My spiritual daughters asked me to close this book with a personal letter that they have found to be so helpful:

April 1983

My dear daughters,

For the coming time when some of you might have to go through dark hours of inner conflict, hardships, difficulties and perhaps other sufferings of a more severe nature, I would like to greet you with some watchwords, which I pray will be a help for you then. These three words have been like a firm staff in my hand, enabling me to walk through the "vale of tears" here below. The first one is part of a hymn verse:

> Naught can befall me that God did not choose
> And that would not serve to my ultimate good.
>
> Paul Fleming 1609-1640

The other two are Bible verses, which I have often shared with you:

> It is the Lord! (John 21:7);

and

> He is wonderful in counsel,
> and excellent in wisdom (Isaiah 28:29).

The Hidden Treasure in Suffering

These three verses work wonders. I have tried them out and seen how they change everything. They are so much a part of me that they immediately ring out in my heart when distress or suffering enter my life, when grave news reaches me, or when burdens and unsolved problems threaten to get me down.

The word, "Naught can befall me that God did not choose and that would not serve to my ultimate good" contains wonder-working power, because it makes us ask, "Who is it that chooses what is to happen to me?" Yes, who is it? Our Father in heaven, our dearly beloved Father. And not some despot who in his omnipotence does with us as he pleases or who deals with us in an arbitrary manner. In overflowing love my Father plans everything that is to happen to me. This means that He thinks about everything — including the hard things — that will come into my life and the next twenty-four hours. What it will be, how and why it will come, and who His instruments will be — all this has been taken into consideration. He has planned what will be good and wholesome for me. Everything that happens to me is conceived in His loving heart. Yes, there is a loving purpose behind it all.

This assurance can relieve our distress and set our minds at ease. For is it not wonderful to know that when a person hurts me or makes me suffer, when troubles arise in my family or I fall ill, when my hopes and plans are frustrated or I am faced with trials and temptations — ultimately it is not a particular person, nor the circumstances, nor a series of events that are responsible! No, it all comes from the hand of our loving Father in heaven.

The second word, "It is the Lord!", tells me that when sufferings, difficulties and unexpected trials enter my life, in reality it is the Lord who is knocking at my door — my Lord Jesus. He loves me and wants to come to me through my troubles. And if you are having troubles now, He will do the same for you. Oh, don't you see

Him? Don't you recognize Him? Or are you feeling dis-
couraged like the disciples at the Sea of Galilee after
Jesus' resurrection? They were in a distressing situation.
Their Lord Jesus was no longer with them. For His sake
they had given up their jobs and everything else; and
now they were without a livelihood. Things had even
reached the point that they had no more to eat. Their
only hope was that they would have a good catch of fish.
Yet even that failed. It seemed as though God were
against them in everything, for they received no help.
Why did the Lord lead them into this distressing situation? — Only so that they would have an encounter with
Him!

But who was it that realized it was the Lord asking
them, "Children, have you any food" (John 21:5 RAV)?
John, because he truly loved Jesus. He knew it must be
Him. Such loving words could only come from the lips of
our Lord Jesus. "Children" He calls them. He is even
more tender in His expressions than during the three
years when He wandered with them throughout the
country. And now He asks whether they have something to eat. Although He no longer has an earthly body,
our risen Lord is anxious to know how His disciples are
faring and whether they are in need. This is the moment
when He draws near. But, apart from John, the disciples
fail to recognize the Lord; they do not perceive His love —
and often we are the same.

Oh, may the Lord open our eyes to see His love, so
that we can say in the midst of our troubles, "It is the
Lord! When I am in distress, His love draws Him to me."
At such times it is as if the Lord were asking, "My child,
are you lacking something? I, the Lord, am here, right beside you and ready to help you. And you will see that
your troubles are transformed into a wonderful experience of God, for I come to you in the midst of your troubles. Trust in Me. Fix your eyes on Me and no longer on
people and circumstances. I, Jesus, want you to see Me,
yes, receive Me and show Me love. When troubles arise,

remember that they bring Me to you. Indeed, when your troubles began I was on My way to you and now I am beside you, ready to help you — only you don't see Me. Let Me open your eyes for you so that you can see that it is I, the Lord, who have come to you. It is not this particular hardship. It is not that person who makes life difficult for you."

That word of John, "It is the Lord!" changed everything back then. And for years now I have discovered that whenever I say this in the face of difficulties, a transformation comes about. I am comforted and my heart is filled with peace and trust.

The other source from which I have drawn help time and again is the knowledge that my troubles are linked with a very wonderful purpose of God. "He is wonderful in counsel, and excellent in wisdom." According to His divine counsels He is actually leading me to a glorious goal — by way of my troubles. Yes, His counsels are wonderful. In times of deep suffering I have found this to be true. What a comfort it is to know that there is a purpose to the particular suffering that has come into my life! — a purpose conceived in the heart of God, who is eternal Love. A great treasure lies hidden in suffering (though often I do not discover this till afterwards), for God's thoughts are infinitely higher than mine. Looking back on a long life, I can only worship the Lord, saying, "Though Your leadings were often painful, You led everything to a wonderful goal — in a way that fills me with awe and wonder. Whenever You destroyed, You created something new out of the ruins." His blows were blows of love. Through them the Lord wanted to refine me and prepare me for heaven. In accordance with His divine counsels, complicated situations were sorted out and solutions were found to great problems and difficulties — though sometimes years later — in a very wonderful way.

Having experienced this so often, I can remain at peace when faced with fresh troubles or unsolved problems. My heart rings with the triumphant assurance, "Your loving counsels are behind it all, and so in this difficulty, too, You are leading me on to a glorious goal."

In such situations I feel as though I were boarding a ship called "God's Plans and Purposes". The Lord Jesus Himself is at the helm, steering the ship over the waves. They may rage and threaten to engulf us, but the Helmsman has everything under control. When I have boarded the ship of His plans and purposes, I desire only that which He has planned for me — wherever He may lead me, whatever He may bring into my life and however He may deal with me. And then I experience that this ship lands on the shores of "Glory". Often in this life it becomes evident how wonderful His plans and purposes were. But if not now, then later, when my ship lands on the shores of eternity, I shall see what a glorious goal He has led me to.

So try it out, my dear daughters. When troubles arise, be they great or small, say, "It is the Lord. It is You, my Lord Jesus." And when God's leadings seem hard and incomprehensible, may your response be, "Naught can befall me that You did not plan for me in love, dearest Father, and that would not serve to my ultimate good. And so I want to go this way, even if I find it hard. I don't want to oppose Your purposes concerning me. Otherwise I would prevent You from leading me to a glorious goal in eternity and ruin Your wonderful plan for my life." Therefore abandon yourselves to the Father ever anew, saying, "I commit myself unreservedly to Your divine plans and purposes." By doing so, you board this ship, which will carry you safely over the waves to the City of God.

In view of all the hatred, mockery and blasphemy our Lord is made to suffer today, do we not have the longing to bring Him joy? We would bring Him joy if we were to commit ourselves unreservedly to His will.

Seen in this light, these three words take on a deep significance, and if we make them our own, we shall discover their potential. So if hardships tend to get us down, foster unbelief and discouragement in us, or even drive us to despair, then may our Lord Jesus hear us say every time:

It is the Lord.
It is You, my Lord Jesus Christ.

In the midst of suffering let us worship the Father for His love:

It is all part of Your wonderful plan, my Father,
and You will lead everything on to a glorious goal.

Let us place our trust in Him:

Naught can befall me
that You did not choose for me,
beloved Father,
and that would not serve to my ultimate good.
I thank You.
Here I am.
I am Your child.
I trust in You
and want to bring joy to Your heart
with my trust.

What a blessing the Lord has given us with these verses, showing us yet another way how suffering can be turned into gain!

With warmest greetings and remembering each one of you in my prayers.

Your Mother Basilea

This slight momentary affliction
is preparing for us
an eternal weight of glory
beyond all comparison,
because we look not
to the things that are seen
but to the things that are unseen;
for the things that are seen
are transient,
but the things that are unseen
are eternal.

2 Corinthians 4:17f.

The sufferings of this present time
are not worth comparing
with the glory
that is to be revealed to us.

Romans 8:18

Other books by Basilea Schlink
for your further interest

FATHER OF COMFORT
(Daily Readings) 128 pp.
These short devotions for every day of the year
help us to develop that close contact, a personal relationship of love and childlike trust in the Father,
which we need in order to nurture our faith in Him.
"That book has helped me like nothing in this
world! I have bought 12 copies and sent them to various friends all over the world. I can't tell you how
it has spoken to my rebellious heart, gotten my
eyes off people and on to Jesus."

HIDDEN IN HIS HANDS 96 pp.
An encouraging selection of spiritual devotions. As
we read this book, we shall discover how to experience security in God, and this will return to us as a
source of strength and comfort in times of
hardship.

IN WHOM THE FATHER DELIGHTS 64 pp.
There are times in our lives when God's leadings
seem hard to understand and the heart cries out,
"Why did it have to happen to me? It's almost
breaking me!" Loneliness, perhaps. Disappoint-
ments. A marriage on the rocks. Severe illness and
disablement. Or emotional stress...Yet never are
we so dear to our heavenly Father as when we are
undergoing trials and chastenings. As a wise and
loving Father He brings us up carefully, desiring

only the very best for us. And if we trustingly put our hand in His, we shall find that He has prepared a wonderful outcome to every path of suffering.

A FORETASTE OF HEAVEN
(American title: I FOUND THE KEY TO THE HEART OF GOD)
Autobiography, 416 pp. illustrated
"We turn the pages as we would the score of some great symphony and whether the music is light or whether it is the deep chords that are struck, our hearts cannot fail to respond. The response will be an inner searching of our own hearts and lives followed by love and adoration for our Lord Jesus. The reader seeking a greater fulfilment in his Christian life and service will discover in these pages the key to the very heart of God."

WHAT COMES AFTER DEATH? –
THE REALITY OF HEAVEN AND HELL 126 pp.
One thought of heaven makes us forget all earthly sorrow. But this is true only when we have a very real concept of heaven. This book seeks to paint a vivid picture of the world above. But equally realistic is the description of hell and the Biblical answer to one of today's most pertinent questions, "What comes after death?"

THE CHRISTIAN'S VICTORY 192 pp.
(American title: YOU WILL NEVER BE THE SAME)
How can we overcome sin? Asked this question,

Basilea Schlink set about prescribing "spiritual medicine", dealing one by one with the sinful traits which mar the Christian's life, helping us to recognize them in ourselves, and points out the remedy. We *can* be transformed by gaining victory over our sins in the power of Jesus Christ, our risen Lord and Saviour.

REPENTANCE — THE JOY-FILLED LIFE 96 pp.
Repentance — a golden key that opens the door to a joy-filled life. It has power to transform hearts and situations.

MY ALL FOR HIM 160 pp.
In this book is described first-hand, vital, all-demanding discipleship, but not as an ideal possible only to the few — for it depends not upon our abilities but upon our Lord's love burning in our hearts.
"I just had to write to tell you how much your book *My All for Him* means to me. I cannot go one day without it and take it everywhere with me on my trips. It is the most beautiful book I have ever read, and I long for a deeper understanding of this Bridal Love."
"Your book aroused and increased my love for Jesus with each page read and made me feel His reality vividly."